YOU DON'T FIT IN

*Because the Surface World
Cannot Handle
Discerning Minds*

Children's Edition
A True Book for Kids Who Feel Deeply
and See What Others Miss

Sahar Soltani

This book is a work of nonfiction. All insights, illustrations, and experiences are based on real-life reflections adapted for younger readers. It is intended to inform, affirm, and inspire children who feel deeply and notice what others miss.

Published by The Quiet Seer Press
Email: quietseerpress@outlook.com
Cover and Interior Design by Sahar Soltani
First Edition. 2025
Children's Edition

This book is produced and distributed through multiple platforms and may be printed at various locations around the world, depending on the retailer or distributor.
ISBN: 9798287757755

Note: This children's edition intentionally uses Canadian spelling and British punctuation conventions, as it was originally prepared for school distribution in Canada.

Disclaimer: This book is intended to inspire and affirm children who feel deeply and notice what others miss. It is not a substitute for professional counseling, medical advice, or parental guidance. If a child is struggling with persistent sadness, bullying, or emotional distress, we encourage reaching out to a caring, trustworthy adult such as a parent, teacher, counselor, or mentor who will listen and offer help.

For the kids **who feel everything**
and wonder if that's a flaw.
It's not.

For the ones who notice more,
think deeper,
feel deeper,
and sometimes stay quiet
because
they don't fit in
this book is
for **you.**

For those who don't feel that way,
**may this help you see
the beauty**
in those who do.

And to the parents
who once feared
their child was
"too much",
may you come to see
it was never a flaw,
but
**a gift
in disguise**.

S.S.

Table of Contents

Note to Grown-ups

This book
is not made to explain
but to uncover.

It's written in poetic prose,
not just for beauty,
but because it carries truth
in the way it flows:
with rhythm,
with reverence,
with room to breathe.

If your child feels everything
and you've wondered if it's a flaw,
this is for you.

If they notice what others overlook,
if they cry when no one else does,
if they question what others obey,
they're not too much.
They're **too aware**
for a world that moves too fast.

That sensitivity
is not a weakness.
It's early wisdom,
emotional intelligence
the world often silences
while trying to bloom.

And it matters.
Because when sensitivity is dismissed,
mental health can suffer.
When deep-feeling children
are told to toughen up,
they begin to shut down.

This book is a reminder:
they don't need to be fixed.
They need to be understood.
Protected.
Seen
for who they truly are.

And if your child isn't like this,
this book is still for you,
to help **teach the kind of honour**
that **protects what's rare
in others**.

Because the quiet ones,
the ones who reflect,
the ones who feel,
they're not behind.

They're ahead
in ways the surface world
doesn't yet understand.

And they need
their someone,

the one meant
to protect their depth

before the world
teaches them
to silence it.

So if you're holding this book,
know that it found you for a reason.

Because maybe *you*
were once the child
who saw too much
and felt too deep,

and now it's your turn
to protect
what no one protected
in you.

Chapter 1: You Feel Deeply

Some people cry
when others laugh.
Some notice small things:
a word,
a glance,
a silence
that everyone else misses.

If that's you,
you might have been told
you're *too sensitive*.

But the truth is:
you feel deeply
because you were meant to.

You were born
with **a heart that hears**
what isn't being said.
A mind that sees
what doesn't seem wrong
to anyone else
but still feels off to you.

That's not a weakness.
It's a strength
that this world doesn't always understand.

When you're around noise,

you feel tired.
When someone is hurt,
you feel it too.
When something's unfair,
it stays with you.

Others might move on quickly.
But you carry it.

Not because you're broken.
But because you were made
to care.

This kind of caring isn't easy.
It can make you feel lonely.
It can make you question yourself.
It can even make you want to stop feeling
altogether.

But don't.

Because the world needs
people like you,
people who feel.

You were **never too much**.
You were always enough.
Exactly as you are.

Chapter 2: Being Loud Doesn't Mean Power

Some people speak the loudest
and get the most attention.
They act like they know everything:
like they should lead,
decide,
and define what's "normal."

But being loud
doesn't always mean being right.
And being quiet
doesn't mean you're wrong.

Sometimes, the ones who shout the most
are hiding something.
And sometimes,
the quietest person in the room
sees the most.

Don't let volume fool you.
Truth isn't always loud.
And confidence
doesn't always look like talking nonstop.

You don't have to compete with noise
to know what's true.
Your calm
isn't weakness.

It's power
the kind that listens
and watches
and understands.

Let others be loud if they want.
But don't forget:
your strength
might be in your stillness.
And your insight
might be the wisdom they all missed.

It's **the same in animals
and nature**, too.

Did you know
that lions don't roar all day?

They don't need to.

They watch.
They wait.
They move only when it matters.

And still,
every creature knows
they are powerful.

Not because they shout,
but because of how they carry themselves.

The lion doesn't need a spotlight.
It doesn't need to prove its strength.
Its calm is its strength.
Its silence is its presence.

It doesn't copy.
It doesn't chase.
It just walks
and the earth listens.

Sometimes, the strongest one
is the quiet one
who doesn't need to prove it.

The owl doesn't shout.
But it sees in the dark
when no one else can.

The deer doesn't push its way forward.
But it senses danger
before it even arrives.

The trees don't talk at all
yet they stand tall
through every storm.

Not everything strong has to be loud.
Not everything wise has to speak first.

Stillness
can be **strength**.

Silence
can be **smart**.
Observation
can be a kind of **power**
most people miss.

So if you're the quiet one,
the calm one,
the watcher,
don't ever think you're less.

It might just mean
you see what others don't.

And sometimes,
true strength
is only revealed
in quietness and restraint.

That's not noise.
That's confidence.
And that kind of power
doesn't have to shout.

And that's what **real power** looks like.

Chapter 3: Sensitivity Is a Strength

You notice things.
A change in someone's tone.
A quiet sigh.
A look that didn't match the smile.

You feel things others don't.
You sense when something's wrong,
even when no one says it.

That's called sensitivity.
And it's not a flaw.
It's a strength.

It means your heart is awake.
It means your soul is paying attention.
It means you're tuned in
to the things that truly matter:
kindness, truth, pain, silence.

The world often tells sensitive people
to "toughen up,"
to "stop overreacting,"
to "get over it."

But what if the world is wrong?
What if feeling deeply
isn't something to fix
but something to honour?

People who feel
make great protectors.
Great thinkers.
Great friends.
They see what needs healing.
They notice what needs changing.

If you're sensitive,
don't shrink.
You were never meant
to harden your heart
just to blend in.

Let your strength
be the kind that feels.
And the kind that cares anyway.
Even when it hurts.
Even when it's hard.

You are strong.
Not in spite of your sensitivity,
but because of it.

Chapter 4: Not Everyone Will Understand You

Sometimes you'll share how you feel
and they won't get it.
You'll point something out
and they'll say it's not a big deal.

You might ask a question
that others don't want to answer.
Or say something true
but they get upset instead.

They might laugh.
Ignore you.
Say you're being dramatic.

But here's what they don't see:
you're not trying to cause trouble.
You're trying to understand.
You're trying to be honest.

When you notice something's wrong,
you speak up
not to be loud,
but to bring light.
Not to stir things up,
but to make things clear.

But not everyone is ready for that.
Some people aren't used to truth

coming from someone quiet.
Someone young.
Someone like you.

Let me tell you a true story.

There was a woman I once reached out to.

I shared a message.
Kind. Sincere.
Not pushy. Not loud.

I felt from the beginning
that she wasn't someone I should trust
but I still chose kindness.
I spoke gently.
I spoke clearly.

But instead of seeing the heart behind it,
she twisted my words.
She responded with sarcasm.
She mocked the tone I used.

Not because I was unkind.
Not because I was wrong,
but because honesty unsettles people
who aren't ready to reflect.

That's when I realized:
some people aren't loud because they're bold.
They're loud
because silence and sincerity

make them uncomfortable.

Some people aren't ready for light.
They don't want to reflect.
They just want to be right.

And sometimes,
they'll shut you down
because they don't want to face
what you see.

But don't let that stop you.

They might laugh at what you say.
Dismiss what you feel.
Act like your clarity is a threat.

You don't need everyone
to understand you
for your truth to matter.

Truth is still truth,
even when it's quiet.
Even when someone mocks it.
Even when only one person sees it.

The ones who misunderstand you
might not see the gold in you yet.
But the right ones will.

And one day,
they'll thank you

for being the kind of light
that didn't dim
just to make their shadows
comfortable.

Chapter 5: Eyes That See What Others Don't

You've probably noticed things
that no one else talks about.

Maybe you've seen someone feeling left out,
even when they're smiling.
Maybe you've noticed when a teacher
wasn't really okay,
even if they kept on teaching.

You can tell
when someone's heart
is hurting underneath their words.

You can feel
when something is unfair
even if everyone else
goes along with it.

You see things
other people don't.

And sometimes,
that makes you feel like the outsider.

But here's the truth:
seeing more
isn't something to hide.
It's something **to treasure.**

It means your eyes
aren't just for looking,
they're for noticing.

And your heart
isn't just for feeling,
it's for **understanding**.

Not everyone will see what you see.
But that doesn't mean
you're wrong.

Sometimes, the ones who see differently
are the ones meant
to lead,
calmly.
Clearly.
With **quiet authority**.

Let me tell you a story.

One early morning, around 5 or 6 a.m.,
I was walking my dogs
when I saw a girl walking alone in the park.

Most people would've passed by.
It's easy to think,
"She's probably fine,"
or
"It's none of my business."

But something didn't feel right.
Not because she looked upset,
but because discernment notices
what others miss.

I spoke to her.
Gently.
With respect.

And as we talked,
I learned she was 18.
She had dropped out of college.
She didn't have her own phone,
or even access to a computer at home.

She wasn't lost,
but something inside her
was searching.

So I opened my heart,
and my home.

She said she was glad she met me.

I told her she was always welcome,
whether she needed a computer,
a safe place,
or someone to talk to.

Because that's what light does.
It shines,
not by force,

but by **presence**.

It doesn't ignore shadows.
It gently exposes them.

And it reminds people
that they're not invisible.

You don't need to be loud
to make a difference.
You don't need to fix everything.

Sometimes,
being a light
just means being there
awake,
aware,
and willing to care
when others don't.

So don't shut your eyes.

Not to fit in.
Not to please.
Not to blend.

Because the world needs
the kind of eyes

that **look deeper**,
the kind **that notices
what others miss**.

Chapter 6: Truth Isn't Always in the Crowd

The world is loud.
Everyone has something to say.
And sometimes, the loudest voice
wins the room.

But volume
doesn't equal wisdom.
And crowds
don't always know what's true.

Just because many believe something
doesn't make it right.
Just because everyone laughs
doesn't mean its kind
or funny.
Just because no one else notices
doesn't mean you're wrong.

Let me tell you something
you might've seen.

Maybe someone at school
was being picked on,
and everyone else just laughed.
Not because it was funny,
but because they didn't want to feel left out.

You felt it wasn't right.

Even if no one said anything,
you noticed.
You cared.

Maybe you've seen someone being bullied.
You see it
when others go along
and some just look away.
But you pause.
You question.

No one is saying something.
No one is doing something.
But you decide to speak up,
to do something about it.

Even if no one else speaks up,
you know deep inside:
this isn't right.

That's not rebellion.
That's wisdom.
That's discernment.

Let me tell you something else.

There was a time in history
when many believed
it was okay to treat people unfairly
just because of their skin colour.

Most went along with it.
The crowd stayed silent.
But a man named Dr. Martin Luther King Jr.
refused to stay quiet.
He didn't use hate.
He used truth.
And even though it cost him,
he stood firm.

Now, the world remembers his courage.
But back then,
not everyone agreed with him.

Some were afraid.
Some stayed quiet.
Even people who believed in justice
didn't always stand beside him.

He didn't wait for the crowd.
He led with courage.

And now, the world remembers him
because **he dared to walk in truth**
before it was popular.

Sometimes, truth walks alone
before it's recognised.
And the right choice
can feel lonely at first.

It whispers
before the world is ready to listen.

So trust that voice inside you,
the one that isn't swayed
by the noise.

Because the ones who follow truth
even when it's quiet
are **the ones the world
eventually learns from**.

You don't need a crowd
to know what's right.
And if the crowd is wrong

**be the one
who does not follow**.

Chapter 7: Overthinking or Wisdom?

You might not know this word yet:
discernment.

It means being able to tell
what's *true*
from what just *looks* true.

It means **seeing**
what others don't see.
It means **hearing**
what others don't hear.

It's the quiet wisdom
that helps you notice
when something's not right
even when no one else sees it.

Some people call it being "too sensitive."
But really
it's a **gift**.

Sometimes,
your thoughts race
when no one else seems to notice a thing.

You lie in bed,
thinking through every detail.
You replay what someone said.

You wonder if you should've spoken
or stayed quiet.

People might say:
"You're just overthinking again."

But what if
you're not?

What if your mind
isn't spinning in circles
but searching for truth?

Discernment means
you sense what's beneath the surface.
You catch the real meaning
behind someone's smile,
or the feeling
that something isn't quite right.

It's like your heart
has its own ears.
And your spirit
has its own eyes.

That's not just thinking too much.
That's **wisdom**.

A kind of knowing
that can't always be explained.
But it helps you
see clearly

when others are confused.

It helps you ask,
"Is this right?"
"Is this real?"
"Is this good?"

Not to ruin the moment
but to protect it.
To guard it.
To honour it.

Let me give you an example.

Imagine you're in class,
and your friends are joking around,
but one of the jokes
makes someone else go quiet.
They laugh a little,
but you see it in their face:
they didn't like it.
They felt small.

Or another time,
you saw your classmate pretend
she wasn't hurt,
but you knew
she seemed like
she was about to tear up

Everyone else moves on.
But you keep thinking about it.

Not because you're dramatic
but because you care.

You wonder:
should I say something?
should I check in with them?

That's not overthinking.
That's **discernment**.

It means your heart is awake.
It means your kindness runs deep.

So next time someone says
you're overthinking,
pause.
Breathe.

And remember:

You just might be
the one who sees
what they don't.

Because discernment
isn't just about seeing clearly

it's about **hearing
what isn't being said
with words**.

And that's not overthinking.

That's **wisdom**
called
discernment.

And that's power.

Chapter 8: You Weren't Meant to Blend In

Some birds stay close to the ground.
Some chirp in chorus
loud and together.

But you were never a bird
meant to flock.
You were born to ride the wind,
to rise above the storm,
to glide in silence
like the **eagle**,
who sees what others miss.

Did you know?
An eagle can spot a rabbit
from nearly two miles away.
It flies alone,
not because it's lonely,
but because **it was made
to soar where few dare to go**.

And when the wind settles,
the eagle does too
high on a mountain,
peaceful and sure,
resting where others can't reach.

Maybe you've tried
to shrink yourself

to be more "normal,"
more like the rest.

But every time
you try to fit in,
something inside
feels off.

Like your soul
is wearing
someone else's clothes.
Too tight.
Too wrong.
Not you.

That's because
you weren't made
to blend in.

You weren't made
to dim your light
just to match a room
too dark for you.

You were made
to stand out
with grace,
with truth,
with a voice
that doesn't echo
but speaks.

Think of the **zebra**,
no two have the same stripes.
They stand out on purpose.
And that pattern?
It confuses predators.
Their uniqueness is their protection.

Or the **chameleon**,
not because it wants to fit in,
but because it knows when to be still.
It uses colour
not to copy others,
but to move wisely through its world.
It's not trying to hide,
it's choosing when to shine.

And the **arctic fox**?
It changes colour with the seasons:
white in winter,
brown in summer,
not to follow trends,
but **to live wisely in every season**.

You might not be
the loudest.
Or the most liked.
But you carry something
this world needs.

Don't be afraid
to be different.
Don't be afraid

to be real.

Because while everyone else
tries to be like someone,
you will stand apart
one of a kind.

You weren't meant to blend in.
You were meant to be
set apart
just like the eagle,
the zebra,
the chameleon,
the fox.

Every one,
beautifully different,
intentionally unique,
purposefully created,
and that includes
You.

Chapter 9: You Were Born to Be Set Apart

Some animals follow the herd.
They look to others to decide
where to go,
how to act,
who to be.

But not the lion.

The lion doesn't copy.
The lion doesn't ask for permission.
It doesn't try to blend in,
or wait for the crowd to approve.

The lion walks alone
not because it's lonely,
but because it knows
who it is.

It was born
to be set apart.

That's what makes it powerful.
That's why others stop and take notice.

It doesn't roar all day.
It doesn't chase attention.
But when it speaks
the whole world listens.

The lion's power
isn't just in its strength.
It's in its confidence.
It never doubts
that it was made to lead.

And maybe,
so were **you**.

Maybe you weren't meant
to follow every trend,
or do what everyone else is doing.

Maybe the reason
you've felt so different,
so alone at times,
is because you were born
to be **set apart**.

Not to show off.
Not to look down.

But to be **true**.

To be the kind of person
who walks with quiet courage.
Who doesn't need to copy.
Who doesn't need to explain.

You don't need to roar
to prove your strength.

You just need to walk
in your purpose.

And just like the lion,
who doesn't follow the crowd,
you weren't made
to copy the world.

**You were born to be
set apart**.

You may not speak the loudest.
You may not be the first to raise your hand.
But what's inside you
is not small.
It's sacred.

You were made to stand apart,
not with pride,
but with purpose.

Some are shaped by the world.
But you?
You were shaped to change it,
to bring something different,
something deeper,
something real.

And even when it feels like
you're the only one,

remember this:

some paths are walked alone
because **they lead somewhere higher**.

It's not about being better.
It's about being true.

You were born to notice,
to question,
to care.

To carry wisdom
and walk in quiet strength.

Don't let anyone shrink that.
Don't trade your light
for someone else's approval.

You were never meant to hide.

You are a light,
meant to be seen,
like a city on a hill:
bright,
bold,
and unwavering,

so others
can find
their way home.

Chapter 10: Gifts Always Have a Giver

You didn't ask to be this way,
to notice what others don't,
to feel things deeply,
to sense the truth when no one else does.

But these are not random traits.
They are gifts.
And every gift
has a **Giver**.

You were made this way
for a reason.
There is purpose
in the way you see,
the way you feel,
and the way your heart works
differently.

It's not just personality.
It's design.
It's intention.

And the One who made you
doesn't make mistakes.

Even your **DNA**,
the tiny code inside every cell,
is like a perfect book,

with instructions only one Author could write.

Even the **stars**,
burning like fire in the sky,
move in patterns too perfect
to be an accident.

Even the **universe**,
the vast space all around us,
is so perfectly balanced
that if one part were off
by even a tiny, tiny amount
less than one part
in a million trillion trillion,
nothing could exist.

Not stars.
Not Earth.
Not you.

That kind of perfection
doesn't just happen randomly.

It means it was designed
with intention.
It means there is a **Mind**
behind everything.

A Giver
who made it all on purpose.

He gave you this mind

and this heart
because the world needs someone
just like you.

Not louder.
Not smaller.
Not more like them.

Just you.

So honour the gift.
And **worship the Giver.**

Because you are not random.
You were not made by accident.

You were

chosen.

On **purpose**.

Chapter 11: You Were Picked on for Standing Out

It was your first day
in a brand-new school.
Fresh uniform,
fresh hope,
and a heart that still believed
new beginnings
meant new kindness.

You didn't come to impress.
You came to learn,
to sit at your desk quietly,
to belong.

But before the clock even settled
into morning,
hands you didn't ask for
were already in your hair.

Touching.
Tugging.
Inspecting you
like you were a thing,
not a person.

They laughed.
They whispered.
They circled your desk
like a game
you never agreed to play.

And though the words blur now,
the feeling never left.
The sting of being seen,
but not welcomed.
Not truly.

Somewhere in the background,
a voice tried to speak up.
A small one.
Soft, but brave.

"You guys shouldn't be doing that."

But the loudest voices
weren't loud with sound.
They were loud with praise.
Popularity.
Perfect grades.
The kind of loud
teachers listen to.

Because when your mom
stood up for you,
told the truth,
and defended your heart,
the teacher shook her head gently,
smiling as if she knew better.

"That girl? Oh no.
She gets straight A's."

As if kindness and grades
always go together.
As if someone who shines on paper
couldn't cast shadows in real life.

You were told,
without them ever saying it:
Your feelings don't count.
Her image does.

And it wasn't just what happened.
It was that no one saw it
for what it was.

But you knew.
Even back then,
you knew.

It wasn't because you were weird.
Or wrong.
Or lacking.

It was because you were new,
and **already glowing**.

You were different.
Not in a way that needed fixing,
but in a way that unsettled
those who only felt strong
when they were seen as the best.

And you didn't stop being kind.
You didn't stop being you.
You just learned early
that standing out
can sometimes feel
like standing alone.

They didn't pick on you
because you were less.
They picked on you
because **your presence said more.**

The one who looked different.
The one whose presence
shook the room
without trying.

You weren't loud.
You weren't mean.
You weren't doing anything wrong.

But you were beautiful
in a way they didn't expect.
And strong
in a way they couldn't handle.

And that was enough
for them to decide
you didn't belong.

And I know all of this because
I was that child.

Chapter 12: You Thought It Made You Strong

You thought power was loud.
That being strong meant being seen first,
feared most,
and followed by all.

But that wasn't strength.
That was noise
covering something
you were too afraid to face.

You picked on the quiet ones.
The kind ones.
The different ones.
Because somewhere deep down,
you envied something
you couldn't name.

Their peace.
Their clarity.
Their presence.

You thought mocking them
gave you more.
But it only made you smaller.

**You weren't leading.
You were hiding
all along.**

Because real strength
doesn't push others down.
It doesn't need a crowd
to prove its worth.

And if you still think
that being loud, cruel,
or mocking others
makes you powerful,
it's time you meet a girl
who proved what real strength looks like:
Malala.

Let me tell you her story.

She was quiet.
Kind.
Just wanted to learn
in a world that told her she couldn't.

She was a girl from Pakistan,
a place where many girls
are told school is not for them.
Where speaking up
could mean losing your safety,
your freedom,
your future
just for asking for a book.

But Malala believed
learning was a right,

not a privilege
for the few.

She was only fifteen
when a man with a gun
boarded her school bus
not to ride,
but to silence her.

He didn't like
that she spoke up
for every girl
who wanted to learn.

He didn't like
that she used her voice
when others stayed silent.

So he tried to silence her.

He shot her.

Right there,
on the way home from school,
in front of her friends.

Because she believed
books belonged
to every child,
not just the boys.

But the bullet

couldn't kill her fire.

She survived.
And when she woke up
in a hospital
far from home,
scared, swollen, and scarred,
she didn't give up.

She got louder.

She kept walking
not with anger,
but with purpose.

She forgave.
But she still told the world what happened.
Because forgiveness doesn't mean silence.

And now,
because of her,
millions of girls
have the courage
to go to school.

And when they tried to silence her,
they failed.
Because she didn't fight back
with fists or fear.

She fought back
not with fists,

but with truth.

She healed
without hiding.
She stood tall
without pushing others down.

That's what real strength looks like.

Not the kind that roars for attention.
But the kind that rises,
**even when the world
tries to crush it.**

You don't need to mock others
to feel strong.
You don't need to silence others
to be heard.
True power doesn't roar
to scare.

It rises **to protect**.
It carries truth without cruelty.

So if you've ever laughed
at someone's pain,
if you've ever joined in
just to fit in,
if you've ever stayed silent
when your voice could've changed the room...

You still have time to grow stronger.

Not by being louder,
but by being better.

It takes strength
to break the pattern.
To say sorry.
To mean it.

It takes strength
to protect someone
instead of joining the crowd
that broke them.

And when you do,
you don't just change your story.

You become
what the world actually needs more of.

Not a bigger noise,
but a truer kind of power.

And one girl,
just fifteen,
showed the world
what that kind of strength looks like.

So next time you think
being "cool" means
being cruel,
remember Malala.
She was never a bully.

She changed the world.

And so can you.

Chapter Reflections

Chapter 1: You Feel Deeply

- Have you ever felt something that others didn't notice? What was it?
- What does being "too sensitive" mean to you? Do you think it's a bad thing or a gift?
- How do you usually respond when something feels unfair?
- Why do you think caring deeply is sometimes hard but still important?

Chapter 2: Being Loud Doesn't Mean Power

- Have you ever stayed quiet even when you knew something wasn't right?
- Why do you think loud voices sometimes get more attention?
- Can someone be quiet and still be strong?
- What's one time you wish someone had listened to the quiet person?

Chapter 3: Sensitivity Is a Strength

- What does being sensitive mean to you?
- Have you ever helped someone because you noticed they were sad or left out?

- How can your sensitivity help make the world a better place?

- What do you want others to understand about how you feel things?

Chapter 4: Not Everyone Will Understand You

- Has there been a time when someone didn't understand you? How did it feel?

- What helps you stay true to yourself, even when others don't "get" you?

- Can you think of someone else who feels misunderstood? What would you say to them?

- Why do you think being different can be hard but also important?

Chapter 5: Eyes That See What Others Don't

- What's something small you've noticed that others didn't?

- How do you think being observant is a gift?

- Do you ever feel overwhelmed by all the things you notice? What helps?

- What do you think makes your way of seeing the world special?

Chapter 6: Truth Isn't Always in the Crowd

- Have you ever disagreed with what "everyone else" thought? What happened?

- Why is it sometimes hard to speak up when you're the only one who sees it differently?

- What does it mean to stand up for what's true, even when it's unpopular?

- Can you think of a time when your inner voice was right?

Chapter 7: Overthinking or Wisdom?

- Do you often think a lot about small things? What kinds of thoughts do you have?

- How do you tell the difference between worry and wisdom?

- What do you do when your thoughts feel too big or too heavy?

- How can adults help you feel understood when your mind is full?

Chapter 8: You Weren't Meant to Blend In

- Do you ever feel pressure to be like everyone else? When?

- What makes you different in a good way?

- Have you ever tried to change something about yourself just to fit in?
- Why is being unique better than being a copy of someone else?

Chapter 9: You Were Born to Be Set Apart

- What does it mean to you to be "set apart"?

- Can you think of someone you admire who doesn't try to fit in?

- How can you stay confident in who you are even when others don't understand?

- Why do you think some lights shine brighter when they stand alone?

Chapter 10: Gifts Always Have a Giver

- What do you think is your most special gift or talent?

- Have you ever wondered where your gift comes from?

- How do you feel when someone sees and values your gift?

- What's one way you can use your gift to help or encourage someone else?

Chapter 11: You Were Picked on for Standing Out

- Have you ever been treated unfairly for something you didn't choose—like your looks, your voice, or just being new?
- Why do you think some people are treated badly even when they've done nothing wrong?
- How do you think it feels to be kind and still be left out?
- Can you think of a time when someone's presence made others uncomfortable just because they were different in a good way?

Chapter 12: You Thought It Made You Strong

- Have you ever laughed at someone just because others were doing it?
- Have you ever stayed quiet when you knew someone was being treated badly?
- What do you think real strength looks like?
- Can you imagine how different things would be if everyone chose to be strong, like the lion in quiet confidence, not loud control?

You are the light of the world.
A city set on a hill
is not able to be hidden.

—Matthew 5:14 (restored)

Notes

Write your thoughts, answers to the Chapter Reflections, or anything this book made you feel.

Notes

Notes

About the Author

Sahar Soltani is a self-published author, poet and mother of two daughters who feel deeply and see the world differently. She also cares for two beloved dogs, treating them like her own, because her heart makes room for all who feel.

Her books are written for those who don't fit in, because they were never meant to.

She believes sensitivity is not a flaw, but a sacred strength that should be honoured, protected, and guided with wisdom.

Through *The Quiet Seer Press*, Sahar writes words that awaken, comfort, and challenge, because the world doesn't need more noise. It needs more truth.

To learn more or connect:
quietseerpress@outlook.com
saharsoltani.author@outlook.com

Acknowledgements

To the quiet ones,
the ones who feel too much,
notice too much,
and are told they're too much.
You are not too much.

You are needed.

To the parents who paused,
who didn't rush to fix or hush,
thank you for being a shelter
for a soul still becoming.

To Annabella and Xyra,
may you continue to live
not dimming your light,
and being a light to others.

To every teacher,
classmate,
or grown-up
who ever made a sensitive child
feel "wrong"
this book is the answer
you didn't know they were carrying.

And to the One
who made me this way,
who gave me this voice,

this ache,
and the fire to speak it,
every line is a return to You.

Other Books by the Author

You Don't Fit In: *Because the Surface World Cannot Handle Discerning Minds*
The original version of this book, a raw, poetic manifesto for the misfits, the visionaries, and those the world often misunderstands and labels "too much."
It speaks to those who feel deeply, think critically, and refuse to conform to shallow expectations.
But it's also written for those on the other side, those who may not have felt this way but are ready to understand and honour those who do. Because respecting what is rare is just as important as protecting it.

You Don't Fit In (Children's Edition)
A beautifully adapted version for children ages 8–12 who feel different, sensitive, or out of place. This edition helps young minds understand that their depth is not a flaw, it's a strength.

Unmasking the Trinity: Yeshua is YHWH
A theologically bold and poetic work revealing the true identity of Yeshua, not as one-third of a godhead, but as YHWH Himself. Written to spark clarity, dismantle confusion, and honour sacred truth.

The Dogs Are Boiled Alive While the World Pretends to Care

A heartbreaking exposé of the Yulin Dog Meat Festival and the world's silence toward animal cruelty.

This is both a cry for justice and a call to conscience, written for those who can no longer look away.

God, Why Does It Feel Like You Do Not Exist?

A raw and piercing collection of spiritual cries for those walking through silence, sorrow, or doubt.

For anyone who has felt unseen by God, this book is a candle in the dark, a flicker of truth pointing toward dawn.

The Restoration of 4 Ezra (2 Esdras) Recovered for the Remnant

A faithful restoration of one of the most important apocalyptic texts, preserved for those seeking to understand the times and prepare for what is to come.

Mind Game: The Global Web of Gaslighting

A piercing, systemic analysis of psychological manipulation, showing how individuals, institutions, and systems distort reality and how to break free.

The Undefiled One: The Ancient of Days Who Trampled Decay

A bold, prophetic work magnifying Yeshua as the Undefiled One: the sinless, incorruptible Ancient of Days who trampled decay and restored the way back to Eden.

Before I formed you in the womb,
I knew you,
and before you came out of the womb,
***I set you apart**.*

—Jeremiah 1:5 (restored)